Programming Behavioral Experiments with MATLAB® and Psychtoolbox

Human behavior is fascinating so it's no surprise that psychologists and neuroscientists spend their lives designing rigorous experiments to understand it. MATLAB is one of the most widely used pieces of software for designing and running behavioral experiments, and it opens up a world of quick and flexible experiment programming.

This book offers a step-by-step guide to using MATLAB with Psychtoolbox to create customisable experiments. Its pocket size and simple language allow you to get straight to the point and help you to learn fast in order to complete your work in great time. In nine simple steps, it guides you all the way from setting parameters for your experiment to analysing the output. Gone are the daunting days of working through hundreds of irrelevant and complicated documents, as, in this handy book, Erman Misirlisoy coaxes you in the right direction with his friendly and encouraging tricks and tips.

If you want to learn how to develop your own experiments to collect and analyse behavioral data, then this book is a must-read. Whether you are a student in experimental psychology, a researcher in cognitive neuroscience, or simply someone who wants to run behavioral tasks on your friends for fun, this book will offer you the skills to succeed.

Erman Misirlisoy got his PhD in cognitive neuroscience from University College London. He went on to found a scientific consulting company and joined the company Peak in 2015 to help develop effective cognitive training interventions.

Programming Behavioral Experiments with MATLAB® and Psychtoolbox

9 Simple Steps for Students and Researchers

Erman Misirlisoy

Routledge
Taylor & Francis Group
LONDON AND NEW YORK

First published 2017
by Routledge
2 Park Square, Milton Park, Abingdon, Oxon OX14 4RN

and by Routledge
605 Third Avenue, New York, NY 10017

Routledge is an imprint of the Taylor & Francis Group, an informa business

British Library Cataloguing in Publication Data
A catalogue record for this book is available from the British Library

Library of Congress Cataloging in Publication Data
Names: Misirlisoy, Erman, author.
Title: Programming behavioral experiments with MATLAB and Psychtoolbox : 9 simple steps for students and researchers / Erman Misirlisoy.
Description: Abingdon, Oxon ; New York, NY : Routledge, 2017. | Includes bibliographical references and index.
Identifiers: LCCN 2016025340| ISBN 9781138671928 (hardback : alk. paper) | ISBN 9781138671935 (pbk. : alk. paper) | ISBN 9781315616667 (e-book)
Subjects: LCSH: Psychology–Experiments–Computer programs. | Psychology–Experiments–Data processing. | MATLAB.
Classification: LCC BF198.7 .M57 2017 | DDC 150.285/53–dc23
LC record available at https://lccn.loc.gov/2016025340

Visit the eResources: www.routledge.com/9781138671935

ISBN: 978-1-138-67192-8 (hbk)
ISBN: 978-1-138-67193-5 (pbk)
ISBN: 978-1-315-61666-7 (ebk)

Typeset in Optima
by Cenveo Publisher Services

Contents

List of figures		vii
Acknowledgements		ix
Introduction		1
Step 0	**Preliminary notes**	5
Step 1	**Initialisation**	15
Step 2	**Setting parameters and opening up variables to store experimental conditions and data**	21
Step 3	**Executing *for* loops to iterate through trials**	27
Step 4	**Using *if* statements to define trials and present stimuli**	31
Step 5	**Presenting stimuli and recording responses**	35
Step 6	**Saving data**	45
Step 7	**Debugging, optimisation and functions**	47
Step 8	**Testing and 'sanity checks' on data**	55
Step 9	**The basics of data analysis**	57
Congratulations!		65
Index		67

List of figures

0.1	MATLAB as a basic calculator	8
0.2	Assigning and using variables	9
0.3	Vectors, matrices and indexing	10
0.4	Defining strings	11
0.5	Inputs and outputs for functions	12
1.1	A starting template	16
1.2	A closing template	20
2.1	Opening up variables to define the experiment	22
3.1	Pausing the program while waiting for a user response	27
3.2	Defining the size of stimuli and starting the 'for' loop	29
4.1	Presenting stimuli for each trial using 'if' statements	32
5.1	Recording the time of stimulus presentation	36
5.2	Detecting and recording responses	36
5.3	Creating an escape key and jittered intervals between trials	42
6.1	Saving the workspace variables before closing Psychtoolbox	46
7.1	Opening up a 'try' statement	48

7.2 Pairing the 'try' statement with a 'catch' 48
7.3 Creating a function in a separate file 52
7.4 Calling your function within the experiment script 53
9.1 Loading your data and basic plotting in an analysis script 58
9.2 A basic line plot 60
9.3 A basic bar graph 61
9.4 Commands for calculating response errors in the experiment 62

Acknowledgements

I would first like to thank anyone who reads this book start to finish. It is not easy to write a book about programming behavioral experiments without inspiring readers to pull their hair out. I hope the brevity of this book somewhat curtailed that urge while still providing a useful resource for learning. If I have successfully helped even one anxious student to take the first steps towards competent coding, then I am happy.

I am also grateful to my PhD supervisor, Professor Patrick Haggard. He gave me the best environment for learning to program as a cognitive neuroscientist, and offered just the right amount of encouragement: enough to keep me going but not so much to be overbearing. I owe additional thanks to all of the people during my studies who introduced me to a new MATLAB function or pointed out some stupid error I was making in my code. Most of these thanks go to Dr Mathew Salvaris.

Thank you to Elisabeth Engl for being a loyal companion for the last few years and hopefully for many years to come. She attentively checked every word of this book and suggested countless improvements. Without her input, this book would be shameful. Having said that, any remaining errors are entirely mine. I also thank my mum, dad and brother for supporting me throughout the process of writing. They can rarely relate to anything I'm talking or writing about but dutifully enquire about it anyway. A final thanks goes to my friend Nick, who provided a bottomless supply of alcoholic beverages during breaks from writing. Although he has done certain damage to my physical health, it is outweighed by the calming pleasantries he furnished in a London pub at the end of a difficult week.

Introduction

Psychology and neuroscience are popular academic disciplines, and frequently dominate science headlines around the world. At the centre of these complex and fascinating institutions is one humble device: the behavioral experiment. Psychologists and neuroscientists design rigorous tasks to explore human behavior. This usually requires competent computer programming skills in addition to strong scientific skills. Modern-day experiments typically run on a computer, with participants sitting in front of a keyboard and pressing buttons in response to sensory stimuli. One instruction might be: 'If you see a green circle, press the spacebar; if you see a red circle, do not press the spacebar.' For standard tasks like these, the computer must present stimuli while simultaneously recording participant responses and giving feedback. This means the scientist needs to write and run an interactive computer program.

I clearly recall my feelings of dread and terror in the weeks before the start of my PhD in cognitive neuroscience. The prospect of programming terrified me. I had absolutely no experience with coding and no idea where to start. After winging my way through my PhD interview with comments like 'I'll pick up the necessary programming skills within a month over the summer,' it was now time to put my money where my mouth was.

Sadly, my fear led me to continuous procrastination, all the way up until the final week before I started the PhD. My learning was delayed and slow but I eventually developed a strong enough practical insight into programming to know that I could program any experiment if I put my mind to it. In hindsight, my fearful avoidance was misplaced, and I should have immediately dived into existing experiment-based computer programs to work out what they were doing. The one thing I lacked, however, was a good resource to coax me in the right direction.

The aim of this book is to provide exactly this resource. The example I will work through describes the process of programming a behavioral experiment in MATLAB R2015b (http://uk.mathworks.com/products/matlab/) using the free toolbox named Psychtoolbox (http://psychtoolbox.org/). You will need both of these up and running on your computer. These are used widely across academic institutions for programming experiments. I developed and tested the code in this book on a Macbook Pro with OSX 10.11.1, but the examples should work on any system that fully supports Psychtoolbox. Carefully read the Psychtoolbox requirements on their website (http://psychtoolbox.org/requirements/) and check that it is compatible with your system by trying out their demos and tutorials (http://peterscarfe.com/ptbtutorials.html). If you cannot run their demo scripts, there may be a compatibility problem. Their recommended operating system is GNU Linux, which can be downloaded and installed for free (http://www.gnu.org/software/software.en.html). A brief disclaimer: I cannot guarantee that the code examples in this book will work perfectly with any operating system and hardware you have. You should fully test all of your scripts to make sure they are giving you the functionality, timing precision and graphics quality that you require.

I spent a lot of time working through many different books and tutorial resources when I learned to program. Although there are many good books and webpages that teach programming currently available online, there are two critical points at which I believe they fall short: 1) some textbooks are good but prohibitively long with unnecessary detail; failed attempts to learn are common with these resources because people lose the will to follow through and give up too early; 2) some of the resources use ineffective or badly targeted methods; often the milestones are set too high or too low and the exercises fail to teach what people actually need to know when it comes to programming a full behavioral experiment.

This book will communicate the core components in programming a behavioral experiment. It will focus on exactly the things that worked well for me when learning to program, primarily because I believe these are the things that will work for everyone, whether you are a cognitive psychologist, neuroscientist, sociologist, or a researcher in another behavioral discipline entirely. I call this book 'fast-track learning' because it will rapidly breeze through the absolute basics behind programming (and even skip some of the less necessary basics), and get straight to the meat by showing exactly how scripts for experiments are constructed. My aim is to get you over the initial biggest hurdle for learning to program experiments. After that, the hurdles get smaller and smaller, and all further MATLAB knowledge will be entirely within your reach. With a little extra help from Google along the way, you will be able to program your own behavioral experiment after finishing this book. It is quick, simple and absolutely not scary.

The tutorials only directly teach experiment programming rather than many of the other things MATLAB is great for, so this should be your primary interest if you have picked up this book. However, the rules and techniques generalise to many other areas including advanced data analysis and computational modelling. The full versions of the example scripts in the book are available to download from eResources on the book's Routledge website page. The script named 'gonogo_tutorial_predebug.m' will contain all commands up until Step 7, when debugging and function creation begins. After that step is complete, 'gonogo_tutorial_postfunction.m' will show all edited components of the script. There will also be a script with the basic commands on data analysis that I explain in final Step 9 (analysis_script.m).

Whether you are a student or academic who has yet to program for yourself, or someone who just wants to program experiments to run with friends for fun, this book will give you a rapid strong grounding in the process. If you follow all instructions in this brief book, you will be confident in your approach to programming any behavioral experiment you devise. Programming is not a spectator sport: rather than just reading this book, follow the instructions along in MATLAB, type it all out yourself and fully understand the meaning of every letter and mark on the screen as it appears. You will get much more out of it that way. So put aside your fears and anxieties, and jump into an enthusiastic start. See you on the other side.

Disclaimer: The author has done his best to provide accurate and precise instructions, but the reader should assume responsibility for checking that the scripts have no problems within their own work.

STEP 0

Preliminary notes

Looking at complete computer programs can be a daunting experience for people with no knowledge about coding. They tend to look like a jumble of incomprehensible numbers and letters. However, all programs start from a blank page, and every line has a functional meaning that can be translated into a more intuitive language. This book will walk you through building a script to run a behavioral experiment. It will start with a blank page, and then gradually write in relevant commands that will be explained line-by-line. It is important that you work through the book from beginning to end the first time, typing in the commands in your own script as you go along. This book is intentionally short, to allow you to learn as quickly as possible. You should, however, always ensure you know what each line of code is doing before moving on to the next line.

Most importantly, you need to write your own comments in the code as you go along (I will explain how to do this a little later on). These comments will explain the function of each line *in your own words*. Comments are important in programming for a couple of reasons: 1) coding languages are rarely intuitive and you may quickly forget what each line of your code is designed to do without a comment to remind you; 2) comments are good for others if you ever share your code with them; people vary in their programming styles and may not understand your script if you have no comments to help them along. Commenting during programming is excellent practice, so never get lazy enough to skip it and think there is no need. Often you realise the point when it's too late and you find yourself unable to understand your own past programs (I know from experience). Your comments next to each line of code will be a central part of the learning experience throughout this book.

So which behavioral experiment will the example code in this book be based on? It will be the classic Go–NoGo experiment from experimental psychology (you can find plenty of journal papers that use this task by typing 'go nogo' into Google Scholar). I am choosing this particular task because it is very representative of behavioral tasks in general from academic psychology. It also presents a couple of interesting challenges such as recording responses when no keys are pressed (NoGo responses). Solving these challenges provides helpful insights into the workings of MATLAB when it comes to defining experimental trials, presenting stimuli and recording user input.

In the Go–NoGo task, participants look at a computer screen and press a key on a keyboard as fast as possible whenever they see a green signal. Whenever they see a red signal, they need to suppress action responses and press nothing. This can be interesting in many ways. For example, you can explore how participant reaction times are affected by trial history: do people respond faster to a green signal following a red signal or two green signals in a row? You can also explore how probabilities of each signal across the experiment affect reaction times: do people respond faster to green signals when they make up a greater total proportion of trials in the experiment? By the end of this book, you should have your own code for a simple Go–NoGo experiment, which you can play with to explore your own behavior or friends' behavior.

Before we start, I will briefly highlight a few MATLAB basics that will be important to understand throughout the book. Keep in mind that this is by no means a comprehensive tutorial of the basics. You can already find many good resources for this online (e.g. on the MATLAB tutorials web page: http://uk.mathworks.com/support/learn-with-matlab-tutorials.html). If you are an absolute beginner to MATLAB, I highly recommend that you work through these basic tutorials to understand what MATLAB can do. The aim of this tutorial is not to teach the basics, it is to give you the extended knowledge required to script a complete experiment. If you're in a rush, the instructions below should give you enough of a background to at least understand the rest of the book. Give them a go in MATLAB as you read through.

1) When you open MATLAB, you can type individual commands in the 'command window' next to the >> symbols. When you hit return, MATLAB will run these commands. Try some basic maths operations in the command window to see how MATLAB can function as a basic calculator (e.g. *4+2*). This example can be seen in the screenshot in Figure 0.1.
2) The MATLAB 'workspace' refers to the location at which data are stored and accessed. Whenever you create a variable or run a command that returns an output, this information is found in the workspace. You can see the workspace in the bottom left corner of the screenshot in Figure 0.1. You can also edit the appearance of your MATLAB window by clicking the 'Layout' menu in the grey section at the top of the window, and choosing what sections you want to show or hide. I like the layout in Figure 0.1, but, as you become more experienced with MATLAB, you may prefer something different.

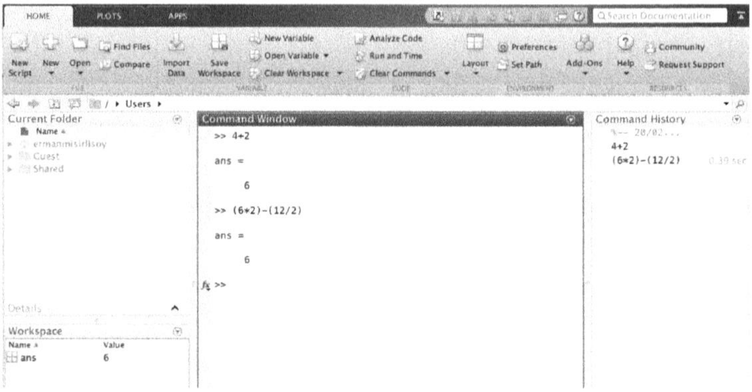

Figure 0.1 MATLAB as a basic calculator (reprinted with permission from The MathWorks, Inc.)

3) A variable is defined by typing a name followed by an '=' sign, and then typing whatever values or information you want to assign to that variable name. For example:

   a) Typing *variableA = 6* in the command window returns a variable called *variableA* containing the digit 6. This can then be retrieved at any time by simply typing *variableA*. If you then type *variableA = 7*, the previous *variableA* will be overwritten with the new value. Typing *variableA2 = 3* will create a new variable (*variableA2*) with a value 3. You can also run mathematical operations on variable names instead of directly with numbers. Typing *variableA + variableA2* should return the value 10 in exactly the same way as if you typed *7 + 3*. You can also specify a variable name to save the output of any of these operations. For example, *outputA = variableA + variableA2* will return a variable called *outputA* with the value 10. See Figure 0.2.

   b) Lists of numbers or matrices can be defined by enclosing numbers in square brackets. Typing *variableB = [6,7,8,9,10]* will return a variable called *variableB* containing a row of digits from 6 to 10 (note: typing *[6:10]*

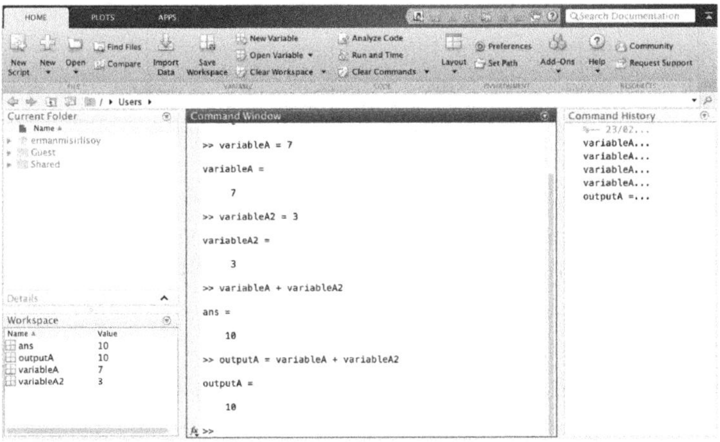

Figure 0.2 Assigning and using variables (reprinted with permission from The MathWorks, Inc.)

gives the same result as typing *[6,7,8,9,10]*. Typing *[6:2:10]* returns numbers 6 to 10 in increments of 2 or any other number you type between the start and end of the range. You probably came across these principles if you worked through the detailed tutorials of MATLAB basics on the MathWorks website as I recommended above). This kind of one-dimensional list of numbers is known as a vector. Typing *variableC = [1,2,3,4,5; 6,7,8,9,10]* will return a variable called *variableC* containing two rows and five columns of numbers defined as each of these digits. As this now has two dimensions, it is known as a matrix. Note the semi-colon operator when defining new rows in a matrix, and the comma when defining new columns. Matrices must always be consistent in the number of columns for each row otherwise MATLAB will return an error. You can view these commands in the next screenshot.

4) You can 'index' particular values within a MATLAB variable by typing the variable name followed by the position of the

element you want to index in round brackets. For example, to pull out the third element of *variableB* above, you can type *variableB(3)* in the command window. This will return the value 8, as this is the third element in *variableB*. When indexing a matrix, you can use two values, the first to specify the row and the second to specify the column. If you typed *variableC(2,4)*, you would get value 9 from *variableC* as we defined it above. Bear in mind again that variable names containing a particular value are treated the same as the values themselves in MATLAB. So if you have a variable named *index3* containing the value 3, then the command *variableB(index3)* does exactly the same job as *variableB(3)*. I define *index3* in the screenshot in Figure 0.3 with a ';' symbol after the command to suppress the output printing to the command window.

5) In addition to the numeric inputs above, MATLAB can take 'string' inputs. Strings are defined by enclosing them within single quote marks. A string can contain any text character. Without the single quote marks, MATLAB will return an

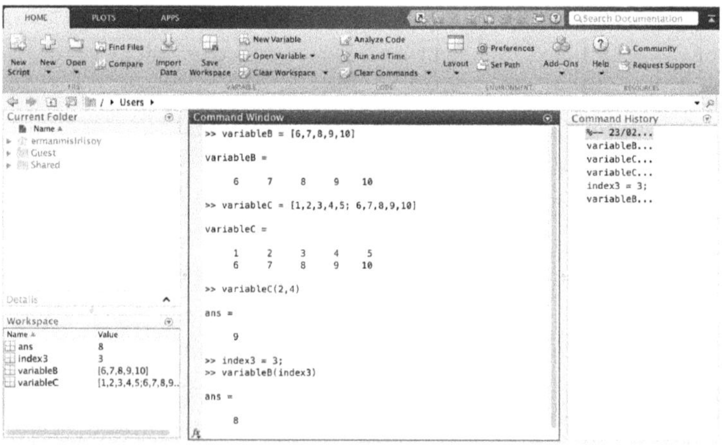

Figure 0.3 Vectors, matrices and indexing (reprinted with permission from The MathWorks, Inc.)

error if you attempt to define a variable with a text character because it can only handle numeric integers and floating point numbers. Any text characters without quote marks are assumed to be a variable or function name, so if the name does not exist, the error message will report that. The importance of strings in the context of behavioral experiments will be demonstrated in Step 1. The screenshot in Figure 0.4 shows how strings can be created and shows the error message returned when forgetting to enclose a string in quote marks. It also demonstrates that you can index strings in the same way that you index numeric vectors.

6) A 'function' is a set of commands wrapped up in a nice little package (for now this is all you need to know so do not worry about details if this is unclear; we will develop our own function in Step 7 of the book). Using the name of a function in a command will allow you to run all the code within that function. Functions typically take a set of inputs or 'arguments', and produce a set of outputs. In MATLAB, inputs are defined by listing them within round

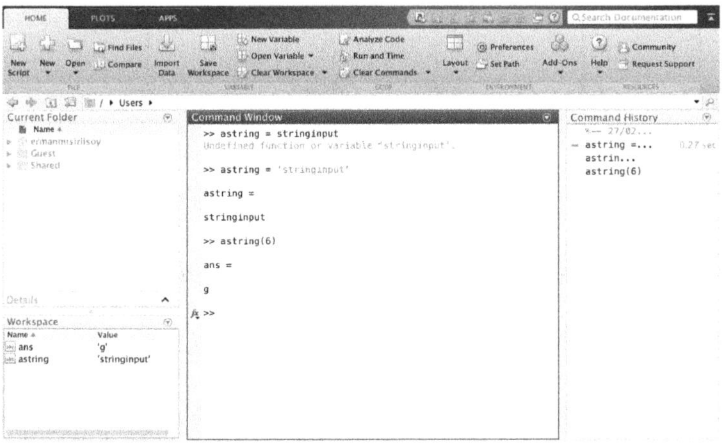

Figure 0.4 Defining strings (reprinted with permission from The MathWorks, Inc.)

brackets, immediately after the function name. The name for an output is defined immediately before the function name followed by an '=' sign (some functions can return multiple outputs and these names would be listed within square brackets). For example, **mean** is a simple MATLAB function used for working out the mean of a list of values. *outputA = mean(variableB)* would give you the average of the numbers in *variableB* above in a variable called *outputA*. The **mean** function will take any list of numbers you like though, as the screenshot shows in Figure 0.5.

7) 'Scripts' are a sequence of many commands that are saved in a single file. They are similar to functions, except that they normally would not ask for inputs when you call them. Often many functions will be contained within a bigger script. Instead of typing commands out individually in the command window, you can type them all in an editor window and then save as a script. Typing the name of the script in the command window will then run all commands saved

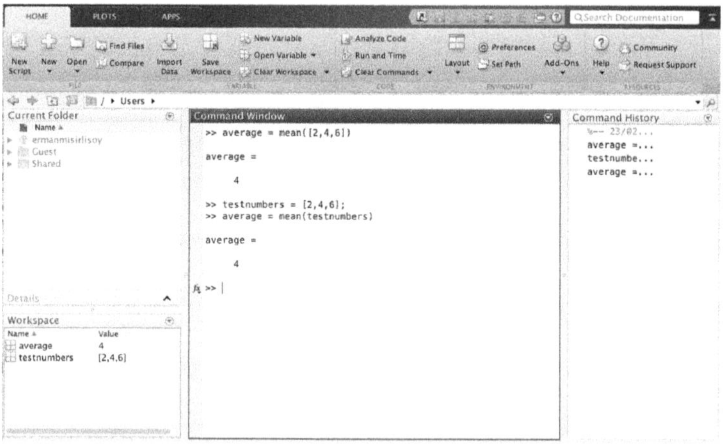

Figure 0.5 Inputs and outputs for functions (reprinted with permission from The MathWorks, Inc.)

within it. These scripts will form a scientific experiment. There are two important rules to keep in mind for scripts. First, as with writing any document, save the script at regular intervals as you go along and make sure you execute a fresh save before running a script so that any new commands are included. Second, it is hugely important to type every single character in the script correctly because even a tiny difference can have big effects. Mistakenly using a comma when you intend a semi-colon, for example, can completely change the structure of a matrix. We will start developing our own script in Step 1.

8) You always need to specify an appropriate working directory for MATLAB when you begin programming. This is given in the address bar at the top of the MATLAB window. The working directory should contain everything you need for your scripting. If you have previously saved scripts or functions on your computer that you need to access, these will need to be in your current working directory before you type out their names in the command window or try to run them through a new script. Otherwise, when trying to initiate them, MATLAB may give you an error message saying it cannot find the file or function you are looking for. You can also permanently add a directory to MATLAB's search path by clicking 'Set Path' in the MATLAB menu. This means that MATLAB will always search that directory when you call a command even if it's not in your current folder. However, it is generally good to avoid flooding the MATLAB path with new directories that could slow processes down, so stick to setting the current directory correctly instead where possible. 'Set Path' can be reserved for when you need to install new toolboxes that MATLAB must access.

9) Typing 'doc' followed by a function name in the MATLAB command window will open up help pages for that function, explaining how it is used (e.g. '*doc mean*'). It

will answer questions like: what inputs can it take? What outputs does it return? Typing 'help' instead of doc has a similar effect but prints summarised help pages in the command window itself rather than opening up a new window.

Here is a final note on formatting throughout the book. **Bold** font will indicate a function name. *Italicised* font will indicate variable names, function inputs/outputs, or other standard scripting statements. Now on to the real action...

STEP

1 Initialisation

We will now jump straight into MATLAB instructions that are immediately relevant to scripting an experiment. I will assume that you have successfully installed and tested Psychtoolbox (although admittedly this can be a little complicated!) Full instructions are on the download pages of the Psychtoolbox website (http://psychtoolbox.org/download/). To check whether Psychtoolbox is installed, you can type *ver* in the MATLAB command window and see whether it is listed). Basic instructions about installation often change as software is updated, so it is important to become familiar with how to find such information when necessary. In fact, there are very few problems you will encounter that Google cannot solve either with a link to a forum or a help page. An advantage of MATLAB is that the online help pages, documentation and communities are very good. It is highly likely that other people have previously solved your problem, and their solutions can be found online.

Blank pages

Explore the MATLAB program a little and find where to click to open up a new blank script page. Take a moment to stare at it. As with starting an essay at school, it is rather scary to be presented with a blank canvas, with the knowledge that it must eventually contain hundreds or thousands of words. Fortunately, the question 'Where do I start?' is easily answered in the case of programming an experiment. This is because they almost always start in the same way with a basic template. This normally involves initialising the programming software, which in our case will be Psychtoolbox. Figure 1.1 shows a basic start to a MATLAB/Psychtoolbox script.

Let's start with a **clear all** command. This will remove all variables from the MATLAB workspace to prevent the possibility that they interfere with our current program (they also remove some other MATLAB processes that may be active in the background, which is why you may see an orange warning message in the script; ignore this for now because we will come back to it). The function **close all** will then close any MATLAB figures or images that are currently on-screen. This next piece of advice should go without saying: please make absolutely sure that you don't need any of the workspace variables or figures before you clear them. If you do, be sure to save them first, because you may never see them again. There is a 'save workspace' button for saving all of your current variables (or use the MATLAB function **save** which you can learn about by typing *help save* or

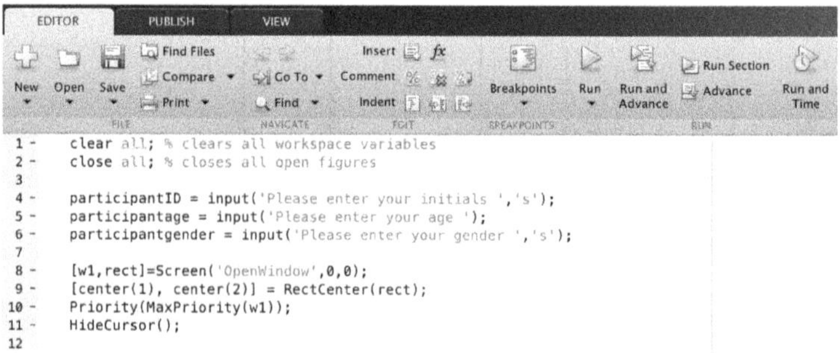

Figure 1.1 A starting template (reprinted with permission from The MathWorks, Inc.)

doc save in the command window; we will also return to saving in Step 6). When you have a figure open, you can use File > Save as to save it to your computer before closing.

Comments

Note that after each of the first two commands, there is a comment included. Comments are entered into a MATLAB script by using a '%' symbol anywhere outside the command itself. Anything after this symbol is treated as a user comment rather than functional MATLAB language (it is usually also coloured green). You can therefore type whatever you like. Just make sure it is clear, informative and sufficiently detailed. The two comments I use in the code above are the only example comments that I will be providing. The rest is up to you. Your own commenting will be a significant part of the learning process throughout this book, so make sure you are doing it in addition to copying out the commands in the examples.

Demographics

After clearing irrelevant information from MATLAB, we can move on to getting some simple demographic inputs from the participant. First, we can assign them an ID based on their initials to keep data anonymous by avoiding links to full names. The **input** function in MATLAB will present its first string argument (if you don't yet know what a MATLAB 'string' is, refer back to Step 0 before moving on or look it up online) on-screen to the participant (i.e. '*Please enter your initials*'). If you want the participant's input to also be treated as a string, for example their name or initials, then you can provide a second argument to the function after a comma: '*s*'. Without this, the data that the participant enters must be in numeric form. After the participant enters their information and presses return, the data will be stored with the variable name defined as the output for the **input** function (i.e. *participantID*). The script above then uses two further **input** functions to record participant age and gender. Age is the only input that should not be in string form because it should be entered as a number, so the *'s'* argument is not used in the function.

Starting with Psychtoolbox

After we have an **input** function for each piece of demographic information we want to record, we can move on to our first function to come from Psychtoolbox rather than MATLAB. If you have properly installed Psychtoolbox by following the instructions on the Psychtoolbox website, MATLAB should have direct access to all of its functions, so all you need to do is use the function name in the same way you would use any standard MATLAB function. **Screen** is a function that you will regularly use with Psychtoolbox, as it is used when we want to perform some operation that affects information presented on the screen. It is a function with many possible arguments or inputs, the first of which always defines what the function will actually do. We will use it here for the first time to open the Psychtoolbox window. The **Screen('OpenWindow')** command initiates the Psychtoolbox screen, which provides the background for all your stimuli. The output variables surrounded by square brackets will return two important bits of information to your MATLAB workspace: the first is a numerical reference to the window itself (here labelled as variable *w1*) and the second is the screen coordinates for your computer in the form *'rect'* (note: if you get a persistent error message for the Screen function, you may have an issue with your Psychtoolbox installation or compatibility with your operating system; refer back to the introduction for more details). The next function **RectCenter** takes the *'rect'* screen coordinates output from the previous **Screen** function, and calculates the centre position of the screen, returning it in the variable *'center'* – the first value in *'center'* is the x-coordinate and the second value is the y-coordinate. You can use this *center* information later when you want to easily present stimuli relative to the centre of the screen.

Finally, the **Priority** function makes sure that the Psychtoolbox window is prioritised on your computer, so that it is less likely to be interrupted when running. Remember that we used the variable *w1* to refer to the window, so this is the input to the **Priority** function. The last thing you want when a participant is doing your task is an irrelevant software message to pop up and disrupt performance. The **HideCursor** command additionally hides the mouse cursor so that it is not visible on the screen when the experiment is running. When the cursor is not needed for the experiment, it is best to make it invisible to prevent distraction.

Templates

When you've typed out the commands above once, you can then use them as a template to copy and paste into future scripts. You may, of course, want to adapt the commands at some point to something more suitably tailored for a different experiment or for your own programming approach. You can find help docs for any command I use here by typing it into Google along with the word 'MATLAB' or 'Psychtoolbox', depending on where the function comes from. As mentioned in Step 0, you can also type 'help' followed by a space and the name of the function in the MATLAB command window (e.g. *help mean*). This produces a simplified information doc in the command window.

Closing Psychtoolbox

At the very end of your script, you will typically close the Psychtoolbox window and remove its priority. You should also use the 'ShowCursor' function with no arguments just to make sure the cursor is visible once you exit the script. These can be done with the following commands in Figure 1.2. Note that these commands will be at the end of the script, which in this example happens to be around line 66–8. Usually you won't know where the end of the script will be at this stage, so you can place these commands anywhere after the initiation commands in Figure 1.1, and then type all other commands between them.

Whatever works for you

So you now have a script with a very basic template for initialising and closing Psychtoolbox. Different people have different programming styles, so these commands, along with others in this book, can vary between people. It is important to look at any other experimental scripts you can find online, and compare the kinds of commands they are adding or replacing. You can usually find existing examples by typing 'Psychtoolbox demo scripts' in Google. This will allow you to be fully informed as you develop a style or approach that works best for you.

```
65
66 -    Screen('Close', w1)
67 -    Priority(0);
68 -    ShowCursor();
69
```

Figure 1.2 A closing template (reprinted with permission from The MathWorks, Inc.)

STEP 2

Setting parameters and opening up variables to store experimental conditions and data

Now it's time to add some parameters and variables that will be specific to each experiment that you program. At this stage you need to think carefully about the kinds of variables or outputs you need during and after your experiment. For example, what kind of data do you need to record? How many trials do you want to run? What are the conditions that you have? All of this information needs to be detailed carefully before you start programming. Generally speaking, statistical wizardry or clever programming should never replace good experimental design. When the design is robust, everything else should be easy. The first step for any experimental program is a strong plan and clear scientific reasoning.

Creating parameter variables

In Figure 2.1 some code shows the kinds of variables that you might open up at the start of a Go–NoGo experiment.

```
nTrials = 10;
numbergo = 5;

buttonpressed = zeros(nTrials,1);
targettime = zeros(nTrials,1);
responsetime = zeros(nTrials,1);
conditions = [repmat(1,1,numbergo),repmat(2,1,nTrials-numbergo)];
rng('shuffle');
conditionsrand = conditions(randperm(length(conditions)));
```

Figure 2.1 Opening up variables to define the experiment (reprinted with permission from The MathWorks, Inc.)

We first define the total number of trials there will be in the experiment with the variable *nTrials*. Next, *numbergo* is the number of Go trials in total as opposed to NoGo trials. In this example, there will be five Go trials out of ten total trials, which means Go stimuli are presented with 50 per cent probability.

Creating results variables

We then define a number of 'results' variables, which will be filled with data during the experiment as participants make responses. The function **zeros** allows us to build an array of repeating 0s by specifying how many rows and columns we want with the first and second function arguments respectively. In this script, the **zeros** functions build a single column of 0s (because the second argument is specified as 1) with a number of rows that matches the total number of trials in the experiment (because the first argument is specified as *nTrials*). Each 0 will act as a placeholder for each trial of the experiment. As the participant progresses through each trial, each of the 0s will be replaced with a value depending on their behavior.

The first results variable *buttonpressed* will record whether or not a key is pressed on each trial of the experiment: it will record a 1 if a response is made or will leave the value as a 0 if the participant performs no action (remember that there will be some NoGo trials). The variable *targettime* will record the time at which the target was presented on-screen for each trial, and *responsetime* will record the point in time at which the response key was pressed (as with *buttonpressed,* it will instead leave a 0 in *responsetime* for any NoGo responses). At this point though, all three of these results variables are a column of ten zeros, one for each trial of the experiment.

Creating experimental conditions

The next line in the code presented above is a little more complex. We want to create a *conditions* variable, which specifies whether each trial is a Go or a NoGo trial. We could use text strings to define the trials, but a simpler approach is to code Go trials as value 1 and NoGo trials as value 2. Numbers are generally much easier to handle. The MATLAB function **repmat** repeats any given value or array a number of times, in effect 'tiling' copies of a variable in a new extended variable. The **repmat** function takes three inputs: the first is the value to be repeated (in this case either 1 or 2 for Go and NoGo trials), the second is the number of rows to repeat it in the new *conditions* variable (it can be 1 here because we only need a single row) and the third is the number of columns to repeat it in the *conditions* variable (this will need to be equal to the number of trials we want for Go or NoGo trials). Remember that you can type *help repmat* into the MATLAB command window to get all of this information. By putting together a single row of 1s as long as *numbergo,* and then another single row of 2s as long as the number of trials left to make up *nTrials* (*nTrials-numbergo*), we create our full *conditions* vector, with five Go trials and five NoGo trials. Using square brackets to contain the two commands together, with a comma included between them, will mean that the results are concatenated into a single row. As we saw previously in the 'Preliminary notes' section, a semi-colon instead of a comma between the two commands in the square brackets would create a matrix with two rows; the first a row of 1s and the second a row of 2s.

As with any line in your script, you can test whether this works in the MATLAB command window independently of other commands in the script (although this can be a little more difficult with certain Psychtoolbox commands that are not designed to run in isolation. For now, avoid testing any commands related to **Screen**). Define your *numbergo* and *nTrials* variables manually in the command window (you can use the same values as in the script), then see if you can run the *conditions* line on its own by copy-pasting it into the window afterwards. You should get a variable called *conditions* in the workspace which contains a single row of five 1s and five 2s.

The MATLAB Code Analyzer

You may have noticed when looking at the code screenshot in Figure 2.1 or in your own script, that the one of the **repmat** functions is underlined in orange, and a message indicator has appeared on the right hand side of the script panel (as previously mentioned, you may also see such an indicator for your **clear all** function at the very start of the script). This is MATLAB's useful 'Code Analyzer'. It points out inefficiencies or errors in your code as they happen. Hovering over the indicator line on the right will tell you what the message is, and it probably says that you should replace the **repmat** function with the **ones** function. Ignore any orange warnings for now, as we will come back to the issue of optimisation in Step 7 later in the book.

Randomisation of trial order

After setting our *conditions* variable, we need to randomise its order. At the moment, the variable simply contains a row of five consecutive 1s followed by a row of consecutive 2s. If this defined our trial structure in the experiment, we would therefore present five Go trials followed by five NoGo trials. When iterating through trials and conditions in the experiment, we typically don't want to present trials in this way. We want to present them randomly so they are unpredictable to the participant, and so we can avoid any confounding condition order effects (for example, participants might be more fatigued during NoGo compared to Go trials because they appear later in the experiment).

To do this randomisation, we should first 'seed' the random number generator so that it's not always producing the same sequence of numbers at a fresh start up of MATLAB (unfortunately computers are not as good at randomness as you might expect them to be). Using **rng('shuffle')** seeds the generator with the current system time, so that it generates an unpredictable random sequence of numbers. The final line then creates a new variable *conditionsrand,* which randomises the order of the elements in the *conditions* variable using **randperm**. When **randperm** takes a single argument, it creates a randomised sequence of numbers from one to the number specified in that argument. In the code above, this argument is the length of the previous *conditions* variable (the **length** function in MATLAB tells you how 'long' a row vector is by returning the total number of elements in it). Therefore *conditionsrand* will index all elements from the *conditions* variable using a sequence of 1–10 in a randomly shuffled order.

Good practice for variable names

Note that all of the variable names specified above are arbitrary and could be called anything. For example, instead of *nTrials,* you could call the total trials variable *TotalTrials.* This makes no difference, as long as you are using this same name to refer to the variable throughout the script. Keep in mind, however, that it is generally bad practice to call your variables something forgettable or common like *i* or *a*, even though some people do this frequently. There are three key reasons to avoid this: 1) you are likely to forget that this variable name has been used already in your script, and then may use it twice in the same program, accidently overwriting the previous variable without intending to; 2) a variable/function name that is too common may overlap with an existing function name from MATLAB or its toolboxes – this conflict can cause scripts to run incorrectly; to avoid this, it is important to create *unique* and *meaningful* names; 3) when you look through your data files in the future, and you see an output variable called *a*, it can be very difficult to remember what *a* means – instead of wasting time going through your old scripts to work out what *a* was recording, it is much better to use a name like *reactionTimes*, which clearly identifies the variable's job.

STEP 3

Executing *for* loops to iterate through trials

Pretty easy so far, right? We are already at the stage where we can start iterating through each trial of the experiment. We can do this using a *for* loop. Before that, let's ask participants to press a key when they are ready to begin. Have a look at the code in Figure 3.1.

Drawing text on the screen

The **Screen('DrawText')** function allows us to put text on the screen. It takes a number of important inputs: first, the window (*w1*) that you opened at the start of the experiment to specify where the text will be drawn; second, the text that you want displayed; third, x and y coordinates for the starting location of the text on-screen; and, finally, the colour of the text. In this example, the coordinates are given relative to the 'center' coordinates

```
Screen('DrawText',w1, 'Press any key to begin', center(1)-100,center(2)-10,255);
Screen('Flip', w1);
pause;
Screen('Flip', w1);
WaitSecs(1);
```

Figure 3.1 Pausing the program while waiting for a user response (reprinted with permission from The MathWorks, Inc.)

that were specified at the start of the experiment. By subtracting 100 pixels from *center(1)* (x-coordinate), and subtracting 10 pixels from *center(2)* (y-coordinate), we shift the starting point of the text 100 pixels to the left of centre, and then up from centre slightly, to compensate for the long string of text. Adding rather than subtracting pixels from centre would push the text in the opposite directions. Getting the perfect position for your text might require some trial and error, in which you run the script and then adjust the numbers until you are happy. For text colour, we here use the scalar value 255, which produces the text in white. If you wish, you can specify colour in other formats such as RGB. Check the Psychtoolbox help documents online for more information (e.g. https://en.m.wikibooks.org/wiki/MATLAB_Programming/Psychtoolbox/Screen_Commands/DrawText).

The function that follows **Screen('DrawText')** here is **Screen('Flip')**. Importantly, **Screen('DrawText')** does *not* show the text immediately on-screen. It simply draws the text on the off-screen buffer in Psychtoolbox, ready to be presented. The **Screen('Flip')** function must be used to immediately display anything that has been drawn on the off-screen buffer. This allows you to draw multiple objects offline before flipping them into the presentation screen all at once.

Waiting delays

Next, **pause** is a MATLAB function that stops the script running until a key is pressed. This means the participant can look at the text 'Press any key to begin', until they are ready to start, at which point they press a key and the script continues to run. We then use another **Screen('Flip')** function to return to a blank screen (as nothing has been drawn on the off-screen buffer since the last **Flip** command), and we finally use the **WaitSecs** function to stay on this blank screen for a specified number

```
circlesize = 100;
circlecoordinates = [center(1)-circlesize, center(2)-circlesize,...
    center(1)+circlesize, center(2)+circlesize];

for trialcount = 1:nTrials

```

Figure 3.2 Defining the size of stimuli and starting the 'for' loop (reprinted with permission from The MathWorks, Inc.)

of seconds before continuing. In the code above, the input to the function makes it wait for one second, but you can change this decimal input to anything that you prefer in your scripts. These kinds of breaks and pauses are important to make the experiment flow nicely for the participant. When testing a new script, you will typically go through a process of trial and error to decide on how best to control the flow of the experiment.

The code in Figure 3.2 will specify some additional parameters before initiating the 'for' loop to iterate through the trials.

Creating your stimuli

The stimuli we will use in this experiment are coloured circles. We therefore start by specifying the size of the circles in the variable *circlesize*. This is then used to build the coordinates for the circles, relative to the centre coordinates of the screen that were specified at the start of the script. The *circlecoordinates* variable will have four values. These define the corner locations of an imaginary rectangle that surrounds the circle we want to draw. A larger *circlesize* will mean a larger circle on the screen when drawn. You can experiment with different circle sizes, until you are happy with the number being used. When it comes to testing your program, you can check the appearance of the circle on-screen. If you don't like its size or colour, simply change the number accordingly and repeat until you are happy (we will come to testing your script later so wait until then because the script in its current form is unlikely to work). Notice that the *circlecoordinates* command in the script above is split into two, with three dots after the second comma. When programming in MATLAB, these three dots allow you to continue the same command on a new line, if you prefer not to have a very long command on a single line.

Initiating the 'for' loop

We are now ready to write our first *for* loop. The command *for trialcount = 1:nTrials* does exactly this job. It instructs the computer to iterate through the information contained within the loop a certain number of times. The number of times in this example is defined by *nTrials*. Therefore, the loop will repeat ten times, as we specified *nTrials* as 10 at the top of the script. The variable *trialcount* is a counter for each iteration of the loop. It will contain a single value, which increments on each iteration, starting at one and ending at ten on the final iteration.

STEP 4

Using *if* statements to define trials and present stimuli

Now that the loop is initiated, it is important to define the information within it. You should always indent information within loops so it is easy to recognise and understand visually (one indent is four spaces). MATLAB will normally do this automatically, but double-check that it works and ensure that it is consistent throughout the script. You can also highlight any block of code that you want to indent in one go, and click the 'Indent' button in the 'Edit' panel of script editor window (if you hover over the button it should tell you what the keyboard shortcut is: for Macs, cmd +] should do the job, and ctrl +] should work for Windows). Now let's go back to the *for* loop we started and start entering some instructions in Figure 4.1.

Using 'if' statements

You will notice in the *for* loop above that we have started using another type of statement known as *if-else*. These are commonly used to define which condition should be presented on each trial. In the code above, for each iteration of the 'for' loop, questions will be asked using the *if* statement. The first uses two consecutive equals signs '==' to ask if the current trial (*trialcount*)

```
for trialcount = 1:nTrials

    if conditionsrand(trialcount) == 1
        Screen('FillOval',w1, [0 255 0], circlecoordinates);
    elseif conditionsrand(trialcount) == 2
        Screen('FillOval',w1, [255 0 0], circlecoordinates);
    end;

    Screen('Flip', w1);
```

Figure 4.1 Presenting stimuli for each trial using 'if' statements (reprinted with permission from The MathWorks, Inc.)

in our randomised conditions variable (*conditionsrand*) is equal to 1. Note that two equals signs '==' asks whether something is 'equal to' while a single equals sign '=' is defining a new variable. This is a big difference so never confuse the two!

Remember that when we defined the conditions variable earlier in Step 2, we coded Go trials as 1 and NoGo trials as 2. The first *if* statement (*if conditionsrand(trialcount) == 1*) is therefore asking whether the current trial is a Go trial. If it is, then the code will execute the indented line contained within the 'if' statement, in this case the **Screen('FillOval')** function. This draws a filled oval with the coordinates *circlecoordinates,* which we defined earlier, and also a colour input. The colour input here is *[0 255 0]*. These are RGB values between 0 and 255. Maximising the green value and minimising the other values means that the circle will be presented in green. This is the Go signal.

Using 'elseif' and 'else' statements

If the current trial in the *conditionsrand* variable is not equal to 1, that means the current condition should not present a Go stimulus. Therefore, the script moves on to the second question which uses an *elseif* statement – this does the same thing as the initial *if* statement but simply presents an alternative for when the initial *if* statement is not met. It asks if the current trial in *conditionsrand* is equal to 2, which would make it a NoGo trial. If this statement is true, then the **Screen('FillOval')** function is executed with a different colour input that specifies red (*[255 0 0]*) instead of green. This is the NoGo signal.

Recall that the *conditionsrand* variable we specified earlier in the script only has two values: 1 and 2 representing Go and NoGo respectively. Therefore, we could have used an *else* statement instead of an *elseif* statement. The statement *else* on its own would have executed its indented commands in any case in which the previous *if* statement were false (i.e. if the current trial in *conditionsrand* was not equal to 1). For now, we can leave the *elseif* statement as it is. It will have exactly the same functionality as *else* and will be necessary if we later want to add an additional stimulus or condition to our variables. If we add several conditions, we need extra *elseif* statements to ask whether the current trial should be presented as one of these additional condition types. Alternatively, if we add only a third condition specified as number 3 in *conditionsrand,* we would only need an additional *else* statement to cover it. The commands would then instruct that *if* the current trial is condition 1, then execute code 'A', *elseif* the current trial is condition 2, execute code 'B', *else* execute code 'C'. The final *else* would always refer to condition 3, as this is the only available alternative to 1 and 2. If there were also a condition 4, it would then cover both conditions 3 and 4, executing its code in either case.

Closing 'if-else' statements with 'end'

After drawing the appropriate circle depending on the condition defined by the *if-else* statements, we of course need to use the **Screen('Flip')** command in order to present the drawn circle on the screen (see Step 3 above). However, immediately before that, we should end the *if-else* statements we opened by typing *end*. Whenever you reach the end of a *for* loop or a set of *if-else* statements, you must indicate this by including *end*. Otherwise MATLAB will be merciless in presenting you with horrible 'ding' sounds and error messages if you try to run the program.

STEP 5

Presenting stimuli and recording responses

We are now at the stage that psychologists and neuroscientists are most interested in: behavioral recordings. In Psychtoolbox, an important function for recording stimulus or response times is **GetSecs**. This returns the current time in seconds, dependent on the operating system being used. By itself, this is not very useful, but if you record the time of different events throughout your script, you can then analyse their times relative to each other. For example, subtracting the time of a target presentation from the time of a response will give you the participant's reaction time (i.e. how long it took them to respond to a target upon presentation).

Recording stimulus times

The first time we will use the **GetSecs** function is to record the time of target presentation. This will therefore be placed immediately after the screen is flipped to present the target. Have a look at the new command included at line 42 of the script in Figure 5.1, within the *for* loop we previously wrote.

The *targettime* variable we opened up at the start of the script will be used to record the time of target presentation on each trial. Remember that this variable is currently defined as a column of 0s, one for each trial (see Step 2). The new command

```
32
33 - for trialcount = 1:nTrials
34
35 -     if conditionsrand(trialcount) == 1
36 -         Screen('FillOval',w1, [0 255 0], circlecoordinates);
37 -     elseif conditionsrand(trialcount) == 2
38 -         Screen('FillOval',w1, [255 0 0], circlecoordinates);
39 -     end;
40
41 -     Screen('Flip', w1);
42 -     targettime(trialcount) = GetSecs;
43
```

Figure 5.1 Recording the time of stimulus presentation (reprinted with permission from The MathWorks, Inc.)

at line 42 updates the existing *targettime* variable by replacing the 0 that represents the current trial (*trialcount*) with the time value returned by **GetSecs** immediately after the target is presented on-screen. As the program runs, this will happen for every iteration of the *for* loop, each time the target is presented. At the end of the experiment, the *targettime* variable will therefore finish up as a column of numbers reflecting the time in seconds of target presentation on every trial.

Keeping a record of target presentation times is crucial, but recording response times is equally important. The code in Figure 5.2 shows how we can check for keyboard responses, and record their times whenever they are detected.

The MATLAB tic-toc timer

We start off by initialising the MATLAB *tic-toc* timer. This is a handy stopwatch function, which starts a timer with *tic*, and

```
    tic;
    while toc < 1.5
        [~, keysecs, keyCode] = KbCheck;
        if keyCode(KbName('space')) == 1
            responsetime(trialcount) = keysecs;
            buttonpressed(trialcount) = 1;
        end;
    end;
    Screen('Flip', w1);
```

Figure 5.2 Detecting and recording responses (reprinted with permission from The MathWorks, Inc.)

then stops the timer to return the elapsed time since the last *tic* with *toc*. Play with it a little in the command window by typing *tic*, waiting and counting seconds for a while, and then seeing how accurate your count was by returning the actual elapsed time by typing *toc*. Hours of fun.

Anyway, by typing *tic* immediately before we start to look for keypress responses, we set the timer in motion from 0 at that point in the script. We can then use *toc* to infer how long we have been looking for a response. In a Go–NoGo experiment, this is an important part of the inference that a participant has actually made a 'NoGo' response by intentionally avoiding a keypress. We don't want our program to wait forever for a keypress in this task because we know that in some cases people will avoid making a response. So, in order to implement this timer for keypress logging, let me introduce you to our first *while* loop.

Using 'while' loops

While loops are similar to the *for* loops we observed previously, except that we do not pre-specify a specific number of iterations. Instead, the loop will permanently run until some condition is met. In this example, the loop will continue iterating as long as *toc* (the time elapsed since *tic* when we started the loop) is less than 1.5 seconds. This 1.5 seconds will be how long we keep looking for a keypress response while the target is on the screen. Why did I choose 1.5 seconds? When targets are presented in a Go–NoGo task, you need to leave enough time for a keypress response to be made, but also enough time to confidently infer that a participant has made an intentional NoGo response when they haven't pressed a key. If you don't wait long enough, your script may prematurely infer that the participant has made a NoGo response when in fact they were just delayed in making their Go action response. Given that reaction times are typically around 400ms or so, 1.5 seconds should be more than enough time for participants to make slow Go responses. If they have not responded by this time, it should be pretty safe to infer that they are intentionally not pressing a key and therefore making a NoGo response. Of course, we shouldn't wait too long either, because the experiment will become unnecessarily long and the participant may get bored of staring at the target. Through trial and error, 1.5 seconds seems sensible, but remember that when you later test the script yourself, you can easily change this time by replacing the 1.5 value in the *while* loop to any number that you prefer.

Looking for key presses

The first command we execute within the loop (remember to always indent commands within loops) is **KbCheck**. This is the function that will check for keys pressed and return them. We specify three outputs for this function: the first output tells us whether any keys have been pressed (1 if yes, 0 if no) but we will not need to use this. We can therefore replace any variable name with the symbol ~ so that MATLAB knows it's an unwanted output. The second output is named *keysecs* and will tell us the time that keys were pressed, and the last output *keyCode* will be a series of 0s and 1s for each key on the keyboard which tell us whether that particular key was pressed. Each key on the keyboard has its own code number which corresponds to its column number in *keyCode*, and these can be seen by typing **KbName('keynames')** in the MATLAB command window.

Remember that the names of these output variables (e.g. *keyCode, keysecs,* etc.) are arbitrary, but label them something meaningful like I do here. Also, you should recall from the 'Preliminary notes' in Step 0 that lists of output variables for a function are enclosed in square brackets.

When we want to specify that the program should look for specific key presses, we can use an *if* statement to specify those keys, just like we used the *if* statement to specify conditions in Step 4. The *if* statement in the last example code screenshot above checks whether the key pressed according to the *keyCode* output variable is 'space', as this is our response key in the experiment. **KbName('space')** returns the specific index number for the space key, which means that we don't have to find the code manually and enter the number itself when looking for the key in *keyCode*. For example, if the code number for the space key is 44, then the command **KbName('space')** will return the number 44. The *if* statement above therefore checks whether the 44th element in *keyCode* is recorded as a 1 (replacing the **KbName('space')** function with the number 44 itself in the script should give exactly the same result). If it is, it means the space key was pressed. If it is 0, it means the space key was not pressed.

Recording user responses

When the space key is pressed, the script will then move on to the indented commands. The first enters the time of the key press into the *responsetime* variable at the corresponding point for the current trial using *trialcount,* in the same way that the time of target presentation was recorded in *targettime.* After the experiment is complete, we can subtract the target time on each trial from the response time on each trial, to get the reaction time reflecting how long it took participants to respond to each Go signal. A final indented command we include will indicate that a 'Go' response was made on this particular trial. The *buttonpressed* variable we specified at the start of the script will record this. Don't forget to include an *end* statement when closing both the *if* statement and the *while* loop.

The commands in the script dictate that if no keypress response is detected in the 1.5 seconds of the *while* loop, then the loop is exited and a 'NoGo' response is inferred. This means that the values in *responsetime* and *buttonpressed* corresponding to the current trial remain as 0 values. It is very important to remember that a 0 in *responsetime* codes a NoGo response – if you later calculate a mean reaction time from the data in *responsetime*, you must therefore exclude trials with a 0, otherwise your mean reaction time may be inaccurately low (more about how to do this in Step 9). As soon as we exit the *while* loop, we need to make sure we remove the target stimulus from the screen by using another **Screen('Flip')** command to return to a blank screen.

A quick note about NaNs

If you would rather avoid using 0s as placeholders in your results variables, you could instead use *NaNs*. In MATLAB these represent 'missing' entries that are *Not-a-Number.* You could therefore use the function **nan** instead of the function **zeros** (inputs work in exactly the same way) when defining your results variables in Step 2. This would create a vector of *NaNs* instead of a vector of 0s, which would prevent any risk of confusing 0 as an actual reaction time because NoGo trials are all coded as *NaN*. Keep in mind though that vectors or matrices containing *NaNs* often need to be treated a little differently: for example, you cannot calculate the average of a vector containing *NaNs* using the function **mean** because the result is always *NaN*. The Statistics and Machine Learning toolbox for MATLAB has a function called **nanmean,** which is used in the same way as **mean** but ignores any *NaN* values. Do not worry about this toolbox for now; we will come back to it at the end of Step 9.

A quick note about redundancy

The *buttonpressed* results variable that we created may be somewhat redundant in informing us directly about whether a Go or NoGo response was made because this should be easy to infer from just looking at the *responsetime* data: when a reaction time has been recorded in *responsetime*, we know that a Go response was made and when there is a 0, we know a NoGo response was made. However, sometimes a little redundancy is useful. For example, after you've collected all of your data, you may notice that your script occasionally failed to record reaction times on Go trials (perhaps due to a bug or some problem with your machine). If you were inferring a Go or NoGo response purely from the reaction times, you may incorrectly think that these failures were NoGo responses. With the *buttonpressed* variable acting as a backup, though, you should be able to detect the difference between an actual NoGo trial and a Go trial in which there was a failure to record reaction time. This could make the difference between concluding your analysis as significant or non-significant. It's easy to become a nervous wreck when programming by including backup output variables and backups for backup output variables and so on. It's up to you to decide what levels of redundancy you are comfortable with.

Specifying escape keys

Looking back at the script, it is almost time to finish the *for* loop that iterates through each trial in the experiment. However, just before closing it with an *end* statement, it is a good idea to have a final bit of code that specifies a particular key as an escape key. When experiment programs are running, they take over the entire screen in order to prevent other computer software from

```

        [~, ~, keyCode] = KbCheck;
        if keyCode(KbName('q')) == 1
            break
        end;

        jitterinterval = 1 + (3-1).*rand;
        WaitSecs(jitterinterval);

    end;

```

Figure 5.3 Creating an escape key and jittered intervals between trials (reprinted with permission from The MathWorks, Inc.)

interfering with the experiment. This is sensible, of course, but it can become difficult to escape your program if you need to stop it while it is running. The simple code in Figure 5.3 will allow us to press 'q' if we want the program to quit.

As before, the **KbCheck** function will check for any keys that are being pressed. The *if* statement then asks whether the 'q' key is pressed (i.e. whether the *keyCode* element corresponding to 'q' is 1 rather than 0). If the statement is true, the code then executes a *break*, which forces the code to exit the first *for* or *while* loop it is currently in (you may need to hold the 'q' button down so that the script has a chance to reach this part of the code – it may still be looking for responses in the earlier *while* loop for example). In this case, it will only be within the *for* loop that increments the trials, and so will exit this and execute the next piece of code outside it, which ultimately leads to the **Screen('Close', w1)** command to get rid of the Psychtoolbox window. The next 'end' statement then closes the *if* statement.

Including inter-trial-intervals

In the script above, I additionally include a **WaitSecs** command outside the escape loop to be executed in all cases at the end of a trial when the experimenter does not stop the experiment by pressing 'q'. This is so that the next trial does not start too quickly for the participant. We could simply wait for one second, but many experiments require randomly 'jittered' interval durations between trials so that stimulus onsets are not too predictable to participants. In the example code above, we create a variable called *jitterinterval* that randomly selects a number between 1 and 3. The first number in the command is the small end of the interval range, and we add to that the difference between the big and small ends of the interval range, before finally multiplying by **rand** which is a function that returns a random number between 0 and 1 (you might think the line seems over-complicated just for returning a random number between 1 and 3, but even the MATLAB help docs recommend doing it this way). We then simply use the newly created *jitterinterval* as the input for our **WaitSecs** function. When this is done, a final *end* statement closes the *for* loop that iterates through the trials, allowing the running script to shoot back up to the start of the loop to repeat the next trial in the sequence.

A quick note on matrix multiplication vs element-wise multiplication

By the way, did you notice the dot symbol immediately before the multiplication symbol in the *jitterinterval* command of the screenshot above? This is not a typo. It's actually required for instructing element-wise multiplication instead of matrix multiplication. In this case it would not make a difference to exclude the dot because we are only multiplying scalar (single element) values. I included it to create an excuse to explain it, so that if you ever want to multiply elements of a matrix together but get unexpected results or errors, you might know why.

STEP 6

Saving data

We're practically there! When the script reaches the last *end* statement after working through the loop for each trial of the experiment, it will be finished. We will have a *targettime* variable filled with one value per trial indicating the presentation time for each target. The variable *responsetime* will have the same structure with the times of each key press response. The variable *buttonpressed* will have a binary code of 1s and 0s, telling us whether a Go or NoGo response was made on each trial.

The experiment may be done, but it would be a bad idea to leave the script as it is and simply close MATLAB or clear the workspace when it finishes running. This is because all of the valuable data we have acquired will be deleted. Before closing the Psychtoolbox window and exiting the script, it is sensible to include a 'save' command. This will save all variables in the workspace, so they can be loaded in again when you want to see or analyse the data. Placing the following save command at the end of your script, immediately before the commands that close the Psychtoolbox screen (see Step 1), should do the job (note: you could place the save function after you close the window, but, as a general rule, the sooner you place your save function the better. If the program crashes while trying to close the window, for example, at least your results are safe!).

```

save(sprintf('%s_data_%dGo',participantID,numbergo));

Screen('Close', w1)
Priority(0);
ShowCursor();

```

Figure 6.1 Saving the workspace variables before closing Psychtoolbox (reprinted with permission from The MathWorks, Inc.)

The 'sprintf' function

Using MATLAB's **save** function will save the workspace to a .mat file. You can give that file a name by including a string input for the **save** command. We want the name of the saved file to vary depending on the participant's initials and the number of Go trials we use when we run the script. This creates a clear ID for the data and also prevents any overwriting of old datasets by always using the same name (unless two of your participants have the same initials and Go frequency conditions, so always double-check!). The **sprintf** function allows you to define a string with inputs from variables in your workspace. By using *%s* to define the location in the string where any string inputs can vary, and *%d* to define the location where any decimal inputs can vary, we build a string that appends the participant's initials with '_data_' and then appends that with the number of Go trials defined when the script was initiated. When you have defined all *%s* or *%d* parts for the **sprintf** function (see MATLAB documentation for other possible formats), you then need to include the variables that should fill those blank parts. As shown above in Figure 6.1, these appear immediately after the string in the same order with commas separating them. The function as specified above will save the file to the current folder in the MATLAB environment. However, you can specify a different directory within the *string* input if you wish.

STEP 7

Debugging, optimisation and functions

Our script now is pretty much complete. Whenever we run it, our experiment should be executed successfully. However, even the best software developers in the world miss bugs and inefficiencies in their programs that require updates to fix. It is very important to check over your code as many times as possible, to make sure it is running correctly with no bugs. It could be a huge problem if your program crashes during testing of a participant or if you discover bugs that have damaged data collection. Until now, the full example script for our commands was 'gonogo_tutorial_predebug.m' downloadable from eResources on the book's Routledge website page. As mentioned in the Introduction, the edits from this chapter onwards can be found in the script named 'gonogo_tutorial_postfunction.m' downloadable from the same location.

Using try-catch statements

The very first step is to surround your code with *try-catch* statements. The function of this will be to 'try' your script, but then execute some other code if any error or fatal bug is encountered. Without this, if your program fails after you run it, you may be

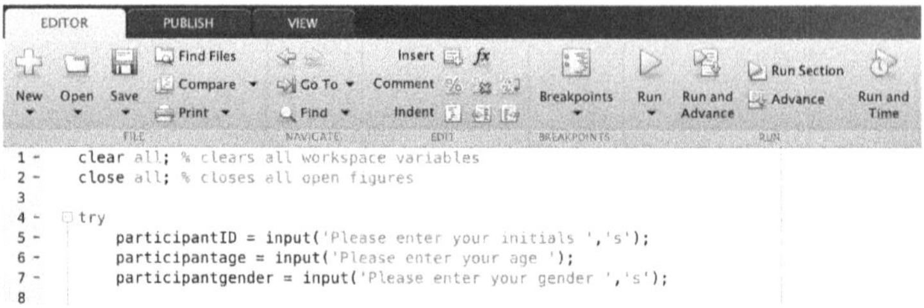

Figure 7.1 Opening up a 'try' statement (reprinted with permission from The MathWorks, Inc.)

stuck on a black screen because the code does not have a chance to reach your 'q' escape command or the **Screen('Close')** command. This black screen can be very difficult to get rid of at times, and might even frustrate you enough to force a reboot on your computer. Your solution is *try-catch*. At the very top of your script, immediately after your 'close all' command, type the word *try*, then indent all of the rest of your script (an easy way to do this is to highlight everything, then use cmd +] to indent the code on a Mac, or ctrl +] on a Windows system). The script should look like it does in Figure 7.1 at the top.

Then, at the very end of your code, type the word *catch* without an indent to match the *try* statement. You'll need to add some indented commands after this *catch* statement that will close the Psychtoolbox window.

You will have seen most of these commands before because they were part of our initial template that makes up the end of a script – in fact, they should be repeated immediately before the *catch* statement that you started. As before, the **Screen('Close')** command will remove the Psychtoolbox window, and the

```
catch
    Screen('Close', w1)
    Priority(0);
    ShowCursor();
    psychrethrow(psychlasterror);
end;
```

Figure 7.2 Pairing the 'try' statement with a 'catch' (reprinted with permission from The MathWorks, Inc.)

Priority command will reset priorities. **ShowCursor** will make sure the cursor is no longer hidden. The new command you won't have seen before is **psychrethrow**. This will present a message in the command window to communicate the error that MATLAB encountered when it stopped running (remember that the commands within the *catch* statement will typically only be encountered if the main code fails to run). This error message will hopefully be clear enough to allow you to see exactly what you need to fix before starting the script again. With practice and experience, you will immediately recognise most MATLAB error messages and what you need to do about them.

Return of the MATLAB Code Analyzer

Now that we've included the *try-catch* statements to cover for fatal errors that freeze our computer, we need to look for other bugs in our code. Fortunately, MATLAB makes it easy to find certain bugs or inefficiencies during programming. Along the right hand side of your script editor, you should see an orange horizontal line. This corresponds to a message at a certain point of the script. If you hover over it, you should be able to see the message. When the colour of these message indicators is red, it means there is a fatal problem with the script, which will prevent it from running. Often, this may be a missing *end* statement somewhere, or the attempted use of a variable that does not exist due to a typo or a failure to define it correctly earlier in the script. When the colour of the indicators is orange (as with the current messages), MATLAB is suggesting a small problem or inefficiency exists. The script should still run if you choose to ignore the message, but it may not run optimally. Sometimes, if the solution is simple, MATLAB kindly offers to fix this for you (if you choose to click fix, double-check the fix is as expected). Other problems may need to be fixed manually. In some cases, the orange indicator message may be irrelevant for you and you can ignore it.

The script we wrote currently contains two orange indicator messages. Hovering on the second message (the bottom horizontal orange line) with the cursor tells us that our script may be more efficient if we replace one of the **repmat** functions at the top of the script with the function **ones**. Clicking on the indicator takes us to the corresponding point in the script where we used **repmat** to define a row of 1s in our *conditions* variable. Because we are defining only an array of 1s, we can use the MATLAB function **ones** with inputs of the number of rows and columns that we need. This will do the exact equivalent of the **repmat** function, but will do it more efficiently. Hovering over the indicator also shows that it can be fixed automatically by clicking 'Fix'. Click 'Fix' to see MATLAB amend the issue for you. Notice that we have a second **repmat** function in defining the **conditions** variable, but this is building a row of 2s rather than 1s. Therefore we cannot use the function **ones** in this case. Unfortunately, 'twos' does not exist as a function in MATLAB, so we will need to leave this **repmat** function as it is.

The first orange indicator message in the Code Analyzer reports that **clear all** may be unnecessary. This is often true because the command **clear** alone will clear the MATLAB workspace of all variables, and in most cases this is all that users want to do. However, in some circumstances, a deeper clean with **clear all** (which gets rid of several other MATLAB processes, not just workspace variables) can be useful. I have noticed in my experience with Psychtoolbox that **clear** instead of **clear all** at the start of a script can impair the recording of keyboard responses with **KbCheck**, which we use later in the script. For that reason, I will leave **clear all** as it is and tolerate the orange indicator message. If you know for sure that **clear** is sufficient in any of your future scripts, then use it to optimise efficiency. Just make sure that everything in the script after that is working as expected.

Building your own functions

The final part of this chapter will go into making your own functions. You should, by now, be familiar with the concept of a function – MATLAB sure has plenty of them and you have already used many. Recall that a function is like a script that takes specified inputs, runs internal commands and then spits out specified outputs. The MATLAB function **mean**, for example, takes an input of a group a numbers, calculates their average and then spits out the result.

The script we have worked through is relatively short and there is no particular need to modularise parts of it in functions. However, in longer scripts, functions tidy up sections of code and make everything clearer to read. Often, scripts also need to run the same section of code at different points. Instead of repeatedly copying and pasting that code wherever needed (and it may be long!), you can instead call a function to do it in a single line. Similarly, you can use this same function within different scripts that you write rather than writing sections of code again from scratch. Functions also make it easy to repeatedly run code with variable parameters that may need changing at each execution. For example, with the function **mean**, the inputs are always changing and may be contained within variables with inconsistent names. On one day you may need to calculate the mean of a variable called *finances* containing 2,000 numbers between 10,000 and 100,000, while on another day you may need to calculate the mean of a variable called *testresults* with 20 numbers between 0 and 100. The **mean** function must be able to handle both of these easily. Scripts force you to 'hard code' the values or names of variables and, whenever you need these to change, you will have to open and re-edit the script. This can be inefficient. Functions instead take whatever input and variable name you give when you call them, and return outputs with any name you want to use.

Although it's unnecessary to use a function in our example script, let's do it just for fun. Take a look at lines 30–2 where we define the size for our circles. There is rather a lot of information in *circlecoordinates*, and if we wanted to redefine this variable at any point later in the script to change the size of circles, we would want to avoid copy-pasting it all. Let's instead make it a function. Open a new script and define a function as shown in the screenshot in Figure 7.3. Then you can simply cut and paste the command for *circlecoordinates* into the function.

To make sure MATLAB understands that you are now creating a function, start the code with the word **function**. Then you specify the outputs you want for the function within square brackets (separated by commas if there are multiple outputs). Then, after the '=' sign, you enter the name for your function, followed by the inputs that you want it to take within round brackets. We will need to enter a size for the circle we want to draw, along with the centre coordinates for the screen; remember that both of these were required to define the coordinates of the circle in the script.

The names of the output and input variables are really just acting as placeholders within the function itself. When you later call the function, you can use any names for each of these variables. For example, it might be that instead of the word *circlesize*, one of your scripts has named its size variable as *shapesize*. In this case you can call the function with the first

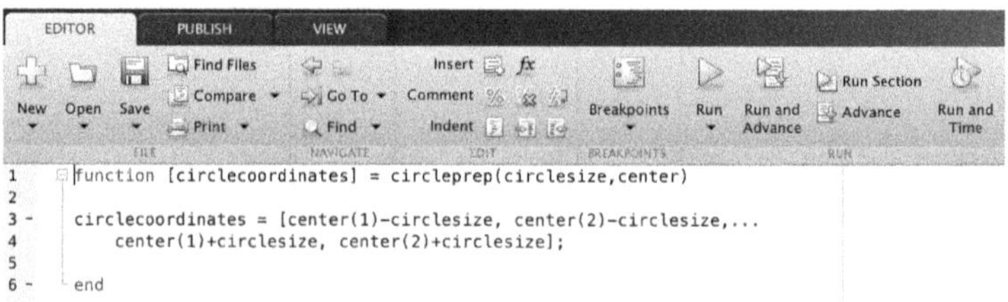

Figure 7.3 Creating a function in a separate file (reprinted with permission from The MathWorks, Inc.)

input specified as *shapesize* without needing to change any text in the function itself, and the function will treat this variable exactly as if it were *circlesize*. Similarly, you could also directly type the number 100 as the *circlesize* input instead of giving it a variable name. The only thing that is set in stone in this function specification is the function name. You will always need to call this function using that particular name or change it within the function code if you ever want to use a different name. The name of the file containing the function must also be saved with exactly the same name as the function itself (e.g. a file defining the **mean** function must be saved as 'mean.m'). Always ensure that the name of your function has no chance of overlapping with existing functions in MATLAB, its toolboxes, or any old functions created by you.

After you have defined the function, you can paste in the commands you want it to contain, and follow that up with an **end**. Now, when you go back to your original script, you want to replace those commands with a call to this function. See line 30 in Figure 7.4.

We make a call to our new **circleprep** function with the output name set to *circlecoordinates* because we need that variable later in our script, and we set the inputs as 100 for *circlesize* (which matches the previous size we had specified for our circle in the script) and the *center* variable that we created when we initialised the Psychtoolbox window at the start of the script.

```
26 -        pause;
27 -        Screen('Flip', w1);
28 -        WaitSecs(1);
29
30 -        [circlecoordinates] = circleprep(100,center);
31
32 -        for trialcount = 1:nTrials
33
34 -            if conditionsrand(trialcount) == 1
```

Figure 7.4 Calling your function within the experiment script (reprinted with permission from The MathWorks, Inc.)

The script will now run in exactly the same way as it did before, but our code is a little tidier. We can also use that **circleprep** function in any future scripts that we write when we need to define the size of circles. This saves us the time required to re-type the long command for circle coordinates. Always remember that your function code will need to be stored at an accessible location within the MATLAB path. It is generally good to keep it stored in the same folder as the script you are working with for easy access. If your script tries to call a function and MATLAB cannot find it, the script will crash.

STEP 8

Testing and 'sanity checks' on data

After the initial debugging, you should go through a final step of 'sanity checks' on your data. We should therefore start running the code. This can be done by clicking the 'Run' button in the editor window or by typing the name of your script into the MATLAB command window. If you get an error when trying to run your script, you can run the full demo script 'gonogo_tutorial_postfunction.m' instead. If the demo script works but yours does not, you may have a bug or typo in your own script, which you should find and correct. If neither script runs, there may be a problem or incompatibility with your system, which you can investigate online with information from any error messages. Just ensure your MATLAB path is set to the correct folder containing both the script itself and any included functions before trying to start the script. MATLAB will be quick to let you know if you forget this step. Remember that you complete the task by pressing the spacebar as fast as possible whenever you see a green circle and pressing nothing whenever you see a red circle.

Often your program may be malfunctioning in some way without you noticing. To make sure the data you are recording are sensible, come up with some process to check whether the data come back as expected. For example, you could intentionally produce a key press response on odd-numbered trials, and no response on even-numbered trials, regardless of the stimuli presented. When you check over the *buttonpressed* data after that (by typing *buttonpressed* in the command window after the script ends to reveal results saved in the variable), see whether the values reflect this. You should see a 1 on all odd numbered trials and a 0 on all even numbered trials. You could also run the script and intentionally produce very slow responses on Go trials in the first half of the experiment, and very fast responses on Go trials in the last half of the experiment. When you check the reaction time data afterwards (see Step 9), it should show exactly this. If it doesn't, then something is wrong. Another strategy is to print intermediate results or variable states in the command window as your code is running. By temporarily removing the semi-colon at the end of some lines at strategic locations within the script (which normally suppresses any printing of output), you will see how your variables are changing over the course of the experiment and you can look for anomalies.

Your script needs to do exactly what you intend it to do. Programs will reliably reproduce what you write in the code, but cannot read your intentions. Come up with other strategies to test your scripts before you go out to run your experiment with actual participants. Try to intentionally break the script while it is running by pressing incorrect buttons or behaving strangely. Did the script behave in the way you would predict it should? Are there representative values in the recorded data? If not, then go back and add or amend code to fix this. You should be able to generalise what you have learned in the code examples from this book to new problems. Almost anything can be fixed with an *if* statement or a *for* loop.

STEP 9

The basics of data analysis

Your script is complete! So what should you do next? Well, the first step is to run through the script a couple of times and have a look at the data. Data analysis is a huge and diverse area, even within experimental psychology alone. A comprehensive look into analysing behavioral data is certainly beyond the scope of this book, but here is a brief introduction to handling the data recorded with your script.

As any good scientist will tell you, the questions you ask during data analysis should relate directly to the hypotheses you had when designing your experiment. Exploratory analyses are not out of the question if you are open about them when reporting, but, of course, the more 'hidden' statistical tests you run, the more likely you are to happen upon a false positive.

Calculating reaction times

So what questions would we typically ask about a Go–NoGo experiment? An obvious starting point might be to calculate the average reaction time on Go trials. After running the script that we completed earlier, you should find a saved results file in the MATLAB working directory. This is thanks to the **save** command we included in Step 6. If your workspace is clear, the first thing you will need to do is load that file back in with the **load** function. If you are in the correct directory you can type simply **load** followed by a space and the file name. This will bring all variables that your script created back into the MATLAB workspace. You can either type this command directly into the command window or create a new analysis script to save this command along with any additional commands that you will include. The screenshot in Figure 9.1 shows what the command would look like in a script for a results file saved as 'em_data_5go.mat'. The commands that follow it will all be explained next.

When the data have been loaded, you can start calculating your reaction times. These are defined as the differences in time between seeing a target appear on the screen (*targettime*) and making a response (*responsetime*). So all we need to do is subtract target times from response times. However, we need to make sure that we are only doing this for trials that were actually Go trials. It does not make sense to calculate a reaction time for NoGo trials. We can do this with some simple indexing. Typing *responsetime(conditionsrand==1)* asks MATLAB to pull out response times only for those trials in which the *conditionsrand* value was equal to 1 (remember that this defined our Go trials when we set up the experiment; all values equal to 2 instead defined NoGo trials). We can also pull out the corresponding

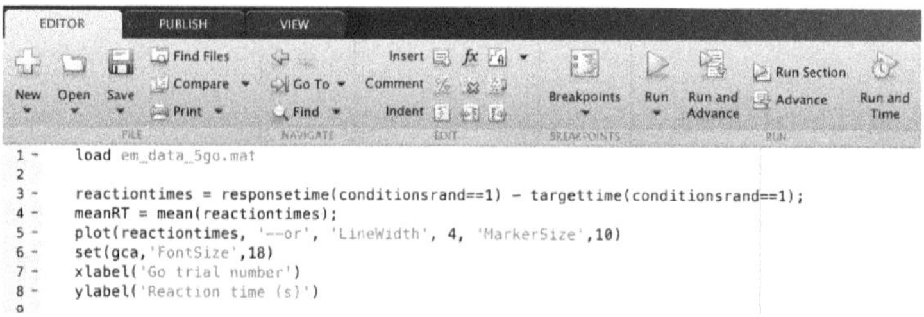

Figure 9.1 Loading your data and basic plotting in an analysis script (reprinted with permission from The MathWorks, Inc.)

values for the *targettime* variable by using the same index (*conditionsrand == 1*). After this is done, the only thing left is to add a subtraction symbol between them to work out the differences.

Once we have the list of reaction times saved to a variable (e.g. *reactiontimes*), you can use the function **mean** to calculate the average of this reaction time array. In the example code above, this mean reaction time result is being returned in a variable called *meanRT*. If you tested 20 participants with your script, you could extract this mean Go reaction time for 20 people in this experimental condition where 50 per cent of trials are Go trials and 50 per cent are NoGo trials.

Plotting data

In addition to calculating the mean reaction time, we end the commands above by also plotting the individual reaction times on Go trials. MATLAB will throw up an image with automatically scaled axes showing how reaction times changed across the five Go trials within the experiment. The default for the **plot** function is a simple line graph. The screenshot in Figure 9.2 shows that my reaction times across the five Go trials were decreasing, so I was getting faster in responding (your graph may look different because you will have different reaction times). You can edit graphs easily by appending labels and parameters within the plot function. I have plotted the line as dashed with circular markers for each data point and a red line colour ('--or'). I also changed the thickness of the line ('LineWidth', 4) and the size of the marker ('MarkerSize', 10). In a separate line I increase the font size for the text along the axes of the plot to 18 using the function **set** (the first input to **set** refers to the object we want to edit and *gca* simply returns the axes for the current figure). Finally, I added labels for the x and y axes by using the commands **xlabel** and **ylabel** with string inputs for the

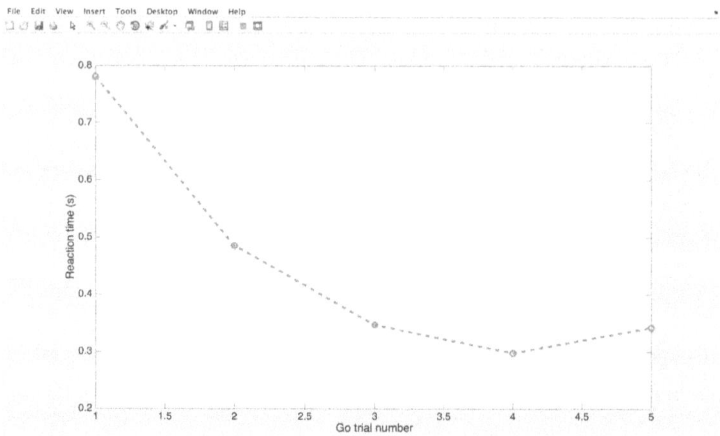

Figure 9.2 A basic line plot (reprinted with permission from The MathWorks, Inc.)

text. There are many other things you can add and edit. Look up the MATLAB plot function help pages or type *help plot* in the command window and learn about other parameters you can append to the command.

You could also plot a bar graph by typing *bar(reactiontimes)* in the command window or within your analysis script (also shown in Figure 9.3 with axis labels). These graphs can be saved by clicking 'File > Save as' in the figure window. Look up the MATLAB command 'saveas' to learn about how to save figures within your scripts.

Calculating errors

In addition to reaction times, we can also analyse how many errors of commission participants made. An error of commission is a NoGo trial in which the participant mistakenly made a Go response (the opposite would be an error of omission – participants failing to perform a Go response during a Go trial).

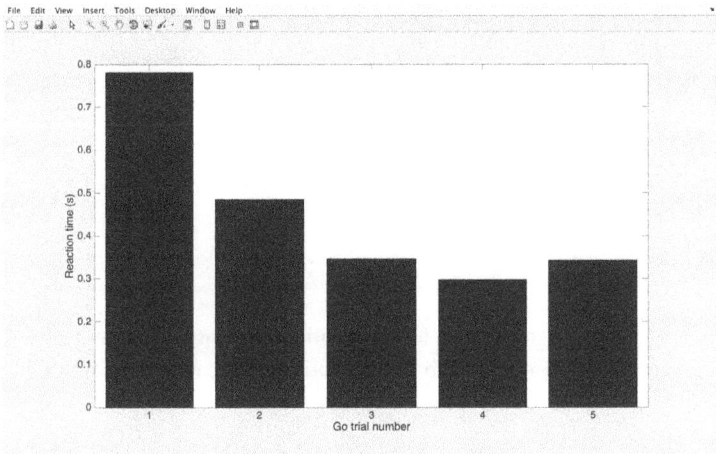

Figure 9.3 A basic bar graph (reprinted with permission from The MathWorks, Inc.)

To calculate this, we need to find all NoGo trials, and then count what proportion of those trials contained a Go response in the *buttonpressed* variable. Remember that we set this variable so that all Go responses were coded as 1 and all NoGo responses were coded as 0. The screenshot in Figure 9.4 shows the additional commands in the analysis script (lines 10–11).

Line 10 is rather challenging to explain, but here goes: we index all of the responses in *buttonpressed* matching NoGo trials by finding the trials in *conditionsrand* equal to 2, then as a second step within those responses we find the indices for all *buttonpressed* values matching 1 (a Go response); finally, on a third level, we calculate the length of those indices to understand how many Go responses there were in total for the NoGo trials. Got it? If not, re-read the sentence until it's clear. The final line calculates errors of commission as a percentage of the total number of NoGo trials. The total number of NoGo trials is calculated by subtracting the number of Go trials from total number of trials overall, as defined within our experiment script. Dividing the number of errors of commission by the total

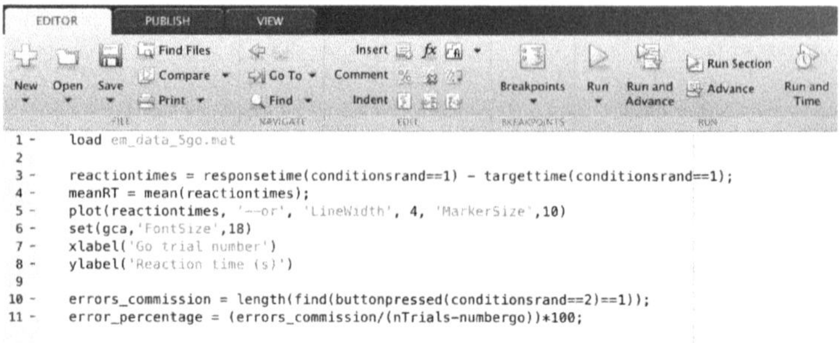

Figure 9.4 Commands for calculating response errors in the experiment (reprinted with permission from The MathWorks, Inc.)

number of NoGo trials, and then multiplying the result by 100, gives a simple number reflecting the percentage of errors of commission.

Comparing data

On their own these data are not particularly interesting (although isn't it cool that you can now extract them with your programming skills?). It would be more interesting if we could compare these data to the same data under another condition. To do this, you can go back to our experiment script and edit the parameters before running again to compare the reaction times you get. For example, you might want to change the proportion of Go trials in your experiment. By changing the value in your *numbergo* variable from 5 to 8 and saving the script, you will change the probability of Go trials from 50 per cent to 80 per cent. One hypothesis might be that because Go trials now happen so frequently, you are much better prepared to respond quickly to them when they appear. Run this experiment and see if your average reaction time on Go trials is faster than it was in the 50 per cent probability version of the experiment.

Of course, another issue you may have noticed is that ten total trials is an incredibly small number. If you wanted more reliable results, you would have to increase the total number of trials and decide how many of those trials should be Go trials.

If you run the edited script on 20 people (ideally the same people used for the pre-edit script so you have a repeated measures design), you will have a set of Go reaction times and percentage errors of commission in a condition where 80 per cent of trials are Go trials and 20 per cent are NoGo trials. You can then test for differences in responses between this condition and the one you tested before with 50 per cent Go trials. If each of your two conditions has a column of 20 reaction times, perhaps labelled *meanRT80* and *meanRT50*, the Statistics and Machine Learning toolbox in MATLAB has a handy function for running a t-test to compare them statistically: *[h,p,ci,stats] = ttest(meanRT80,meanRT50)*. This would return both the p-value and the basic stats (e.g. t statistic) for the result. If you want to use the **ttest** function but don't have the Statistics and Machine Learning toolbox, you will need to buy and install it from MathWorks (remember that you can find out what toolboxes you already have installed by typing *ver* in the MATLAB command window). The toolbox also contains a **ttest2** function if you need an independent measures t-test, and, of course, functions for plenty of other advanced statistics.

Congratulations!

That's all of your nine steps complete! You now have the essential skills for beginning to program your own experiments. Hopefully, this is far from the end of your MATLAB learning experience. In fact, you're never likely to stop learning as long as you use it. There are many possible next steps to immediately build on what you have learned here.

Play with the script we developed together by further changing existing parameters to see what effects they have. You could try changing the *circlesize* input into your **circleprep** function when you call it in the script, for example, or perhaps try reducing how long the script leaves targets on the screen while searching for a Go response in the *while* loop. You could also try adding some code. It might be worthwhile including a fixation cross that appears before the targets. The Psychtoolbox function **Screen('DrawText')** that you have already used should be able to do this easily with the '+' symbol as the text input. Just put it wherever you feel is appropriate in the script and see if it works. You can also use the same function to present brief instructions to the participant before the experiment starts.

The next steps above are just suggestions. The point of programming is that it is highly flexible and powerful, allowing you to do practically anything with your experiment. To develop your expertise, jump straight into writing new experiments with the steps highlighted in this book. Find and understand other existing demo scripts online that are most relevant to your own work, and study other useful functions in MATLAB and Psychtoolbox. Do your best to keep your programs concise and efficient, as shorter programs are generally easier to work with and debug. Keep your programs organised and begin each new script by using an old script as a template for efficiency. Develop a furious habit for commenting regularly in your programming so that you never waste time understanding old code. Anyone who reads your code in the future will also thank you.

Finally, whenever you are trying to fix a repetitive or tedious problem manually, such as typing numbers into spreadsheets or restructuring data, think to yourself: 'Can I write a script that will do this job for me?' If so, then you should immediately open MATLAB and start coding. It may take a while to write a script the first time, but after it is done, you can use it repeatedly for the rest of your life to solve the problem within seconds. You will have one less tedious job to worry about.

Index

accessible 54
analysis 57
anomalies 56
arguments 21
axes 59

backup 41
basics 7
blank 28
brackets 8, 10, 12, 23, 52
break 42
buffer 28
bugs 47, 49

calculator 7
center 19
circles 29
circlesize 29
clear 16, 50
close 16, 20, 42
code 5
colour 17, 27, 28, 32, 33, 59
comma 9, 13
command window 7
comments 5, 17
companion website 3
compare 62
concatenated 23
conditions 23
coordinates 18, 19
counter 30
crashes 45, 47
cursor 19, 20

data 22, 55-63
demo 2, 20, 66
demographic 17-18
directory 13, 57-8
download 2
DrawText 27-8, 65

element-wise multiplication 43
else 32-3
elseif 33

end 20, 33-4
equal to 32-3, 58
errors 24
escape 41-2
exit 20
exploratory 57

FillOval 32-3
fix 50
fixation 65
Flip 28, 33
flow 29
folder 13, 46
font 14, 59
for loop 27, 29-30, 34
formatting 14
function 11-12, 50-4

GetSecs 35-6
Go–NoGo 6
graph 59-61

help 13-15, 19, 28, 60
hypotheses 57, 62

if statement 31-3
increments 9, 30
indent 31, 48
indexing 9-10, 58
inefficiencies 24, 47, 49
input 11, 17, 52
instructions 65
interval 42-3
iterate 29-30

jittered 42-3

KbCheck 38, 42
keyboard responses 36, 38
keys pressed 38

labels 59
layout 7
load 58

malfunctioning 55
marker 59
MathWorks 2
MATLAB 2
MATLAB Code Analyzer 24, 49-50
matrix 8-10, 43
matrix multiplication 43
mean 12, 51, 59
modularise 51

nanmean 40
NaNs 40

ones 24, 50
overwriting 26, 46

parameters 21-2, 60, 62, 65
path 13, 54
pause 28-9
percentage 61-2
pixels 28
plot 59-60
priority 19-20, 49

psychrethrow 49
Psychtoolbox 2, 15
p-value 63

quit 42

rand 25, 43
randomisation 24-5
randperm 25
reaction time 6, 35, 40-1, 57-9
recording 35-6
redundancy 41
repeat 22-3
replacing 36
repmat 23-4, 50
results 22, 55, 57
RGB 32
run 55

sanity checks 55
save 13, 16-17, 45-6, 53, 57-8
screen 18-19, 27-9, 32-3, 42, 48
scripts 2, 12-13
seed 25
semi-colon 9-10, 13, 23-4, 56
set 13, 21, 59-60
ShowCursor 20, 49
shuffle 25
size 29, 51-3, 59
sprintf 46
statistics 40, 63
Statistics and Machine Learning toolbox 40, 63
stimuli 18-19, 29-30
strings 10-11, 23
suppress 10, 56

template 16, 19
test 24, 63
text 27-8, 65
tic-toc 36-7
time 22-3, 35
timer 36-7
trial order 24-5
try-catch 47-9
t-test 63

user responses 39-40

variable 8-9
variable names 8-10, 18, 25-6
vector 8-9
ver 15

waiting 28-9
WaitSecs 28, 42-3
warnings 16, 24
while loop 37-40
working directory 13, 57
workspace 7, 16, 45-6

zeros 22, 40

For Product Safety Concerns and Information please contact our EU representative GPSR@taylorandfrancis.com
Taylor & Francis Verlag GmbH, Kaufingerstraße 24, 80331 München, Germany

www.ingramcontent.com/pod-product-compliance
Ingram Content Group UK Ltd.
Pitfield, Milton Keynes, MK11 3LW, UK
UKHW021501240926
475702UK00035B/92
9781138671928